LEARN KANA WITH *YOKAI!*

WRITTEN AND TRANSLATED BY C.M. ZIMMERMAN
ILLUSTRATED BY SVETLANA ZIMMERMAN

JOROUGUMO ①

じょろうぐも ②

Jorougumo is a cunning and enchanting yokai, part woman and part spider, known for her deadly beauty and deceptive charm. In her human form, she appears as a stunning young woman, captivating and bewitching those who cross her path. However, beneath her alluring kimono lies the body of a massive spider, capable of spinning webs strong enough to entrap even the most formidable prey. Jorougumo resides near waterfalls, abandoned houses, or other secluded places where she can lure unsuspecting travelers. Once a victim is ensnared by her charms, she reveals her true form, paralyzing her prey with venom before wrapping them in silk. Legends say she can control smaller spiders, using them to aid in her hunt. Despite her terrifying nature, some stories depict Jorougumo as a tragic figure, cursed by her nature but longing for human connection. ③

LETS TRY IT OUT! / やってみよう！

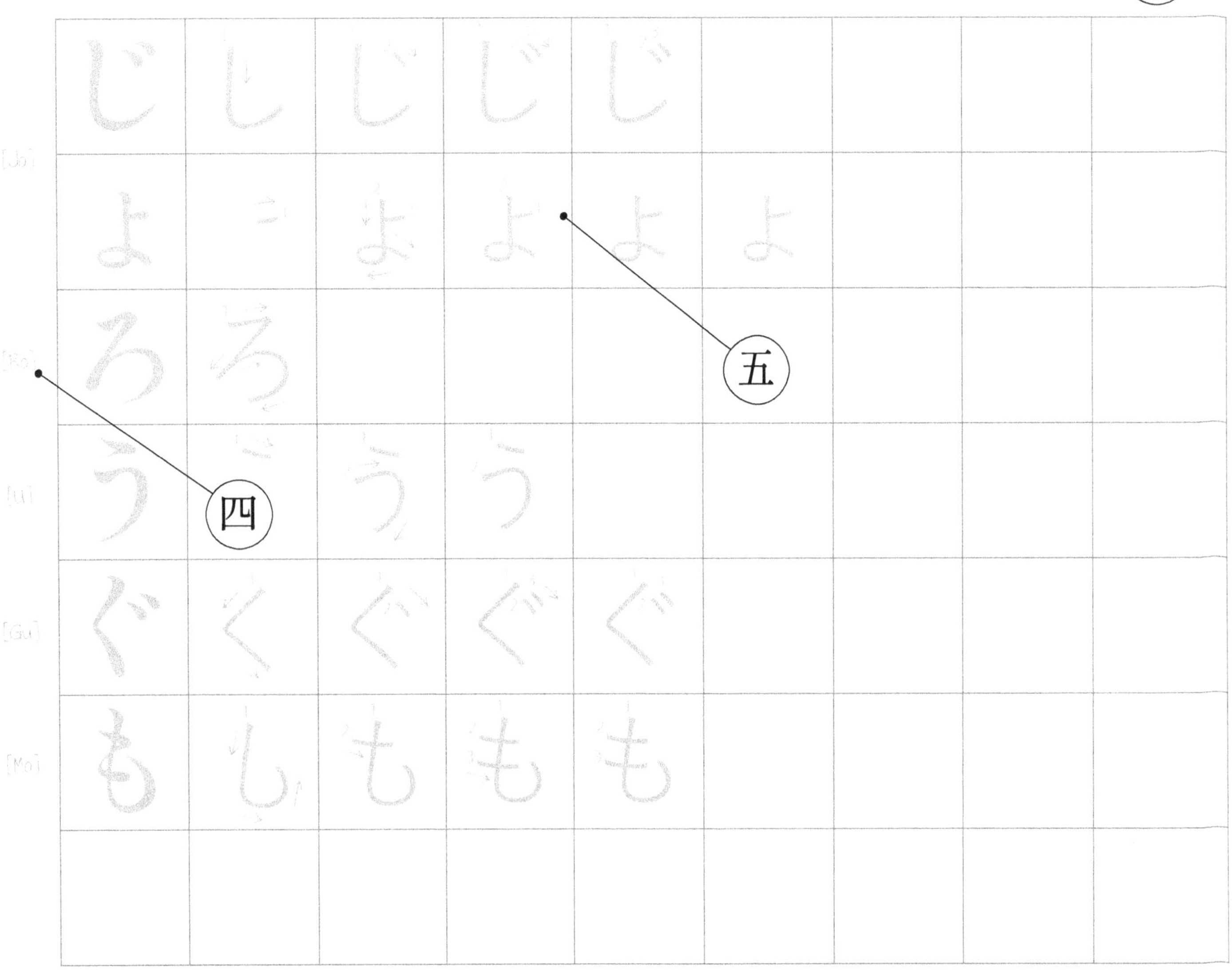

HOW TO USE THIS BOOK?!

OVERVIEW:

THIS BOOK HAS SEVERAL HELPFUL SECTIONS ON EACH PAGE TO AID THE READER IN EXPLORING THIS FOLK LANDSCAPE FROM A DISTANCE, AS WELL AS DEEPEN THEIR UNDERSTANDING OF THE IMAGES THAT WERE INSPIRED BY ITS BEAUTY. BEYOND THE STUNNING ARTWORK THAT AWAITS YOU THROUGHOUT THE BOOK, YOU MIGHT ALSO LIKE TO LEARN A BIT ABOUT THE CULTURE, THE HISTORY AND THE LANGUAGE THAT BROUGHT FORTH THESE FASCINATING CREATURES INTO OUR WORLD!

THEREFORE ON EVERY PAGE YOU CAN:

一) LEARN THE ENGLISH PRONUNCIATION OF THE YOKAI'S NAME;

二) SEE HOW THE CHARACTERS ARE WRITTEN IN THEIR ORIGINAL LANGUAGE;

三) READ A SMALL EXCERPT ABOUT THE YOKAI: INCLUDING CULTURAL AND HISTORICAL NOTES RELATED TO ITS ORIGIN;

四) DISCOVER THE READINGS OF EACH CHARACTER;

五) PRACTICE WRITING THE NAMES WITH THE CORRECT STROKE ORDER YOURSELF...

...SO YOU CAN ACT COOL IN FRONT OF YOUR FRIENDS.

AND FINALLY, DON'T FORGET TO GET LOST IN THE FANTASTICAL WORLD OF JAPAN'S YOKAI WHILE YOU COLOR-IN THE IMAGES ON THE FOLLOWING PAGE!

ENJOY, AND LETS GET STARTED!

JOROUGUMO

HANGONKOU
はんごんこう

Allow me to introduce the Hangonkou, a mystical incense with a bittersweet twist. Originating from ancient China, this legendary scent is crafted from the magical hangonjū tree. When burned, Hangonkou summons the spirits of the dead into the swirling smoke, offering a fleeting chance to glimpse lost loved ones. However, the catch is that these spirits only linger within the smoke, leaving those who seek them with a heart-wrenching reminder of their loss rather than any sort of solace. It serves as a poignant allegory for the delusion of clinging to the past and the despair that comes from an inability to let go, reflecting the Buddhist belief that such attachments are the root of all suffering.

LET'S TRY IT OUT! / やってみよう!

[Ha]	は							
[N]	ん							
[Go]	ご							
[N]	ん							
[Ko]	こ							
[U]	う							

はんごんこう

HANGONKOU

DENPACHI GITSUNE

でんぱちぎつね

Meet the Denpachi Gitsune, the fox spirit with a knack for blending in and causing a ruckus. Once upon a time in Sōsa City, Chiba Prefecture, this cunning kitsune managed to infiltrate a prestigious Buddhist seminary by disguising himself as a studious young lad named Denpachi. For ten years, Denpachi was the epitome of a model student, sweeping floors, preparing meals, and acing his studies while keeping his true identity a secret. His only slip-ups were the occasional fox paw prints and misplaced leaves with Lotus Sutra that led to whispers of mischief—though no one suspected him. However, during a wild banquet celebrating a new headmaster, Denpachi's disguise fell apart after a bit too much sake, revealing his true fox form. The shocked students tied him up and brought him before the headmaster. Fortunately, he was moved by Denpachi's heartfelt confession and dedication, forgiving him and offering him a role as the temple's guardian spirit. Nowadays, he is known as Konoha Inari Daimyōjin, this benevolent fox spirit continues to be a popular local deity, ensuring that even the most mischievous spirits can find redemption and a place in the hearts of the believers.

LET'S TRY IT OUT! / やってみよう!

[De]	で	て	て	で	で		
[N]	ん	ん	ん				
[Pa]	ぱ	い	に	ぱ	ぱ	ぱ	
[Chi]	ち	ー	ち	ち	ち		
[Gi]	ぎ	ー	き	き	き	ぎ	ぎ
[Tsu]	つ	つ	つ				
[Ne]	ね	ー	ね	ね			

でんぱちぎつね

DENPACHI GITSUNE

AO NYOUBOU

あおにょうぼう

The Ao Nyoubou is a spirit with a serious case of nostalgia—and maybe a touch of the blues. Once a beautiful court lady, she now haunts abandoned mansions, her elegant robes and powdered face a faded echo of her former glory. But don't let her appearance fool you; despite her forlorn look, she's more than capable of bringing mischief wherever she goes. She spends her days sulking in the shadows and her nights scaring away anyone who dares to trespass on her territory. If you ever stumble upon an eerie, old estate and hear the rustle of silk in the dark, just remember, never comment on her makeup—she's had a few centuries to perfect that look!

LET'S TRY IT OUT! /やってみよう!

[A] あ			あ	あ			
[O] お		お	お	お			
[Ni] に		に	に	に			
[Nyo] よ		よ	よ				
[U] う		う	う				
[Bo] ぼ			ほ	ぼ	ぼ	ぼ	
[U] う		う	う				

あおにょうぼう

AO NYOUBOU

GASHADOKURO
がしゃどくろ

Introducing the Gashadokuro, the towering skeletal giant that's more about bones than just a spooky Halloween decoration. These enormous yokai are the vengeful spirits of those who died of starvation or in battle, and their massive, skeletal forms are a chilling reminder of their tragic end. Standing at an awe-inspiring height, they roam the countryside, their hollow bones clattering with every step. They're known for sneaking up on their victims and crushing them with a bone-crunching embrace. If you hear eerie clattering sounds at night or feel a sudden chill, beware—the Gashadokuro might be nearby, looking to add a few more bones to its collection.

LET'S TRY IT OUT! / やってみよう!

[Ga]	が	つ	か	か	が	が	が		
[Sha]	し	し	し	し					
	や	っ	や	や	や				
[Do]	ど	い	ど	ど	ど				
[Ku]	く	く	く	く					
[Ro]	ろ	ろ	ろ	ろ					

がしゃどくろ

GASHADOKURO

BIRON
びろ〜ん

The Biron is a rather harmless yokai with a flair for the dramatic. This mysterious creature loves to give humans a good scare by gently caressing their heads and necks with its long, snake-like tail. Though its eerie touch might send shivers down your spine, dealing with a Biron is as easy as tossing a pinch of salt its way, causing it to vanish into thin air. According to legend, the Biron was born from a magical mishap—it tried to transform into a Buddha by chanting "Biro! Biro! Biro~n!" but the spell went hilariously wrong, leaving it with its strange appearance. While its origins are shrouded in mystery, and some believe it's the creation of the yokai researcher Satō Arifumi, one thing is certain: the Biron may be spooky, but it's more about harmless fun than any real danger!

LET'S TRY IT OUT! / やってみよう！

[Bi]	び	び	び	び	び		
[Ro]	ろ	ろ	ろ	ろ			
[Long sound]*	〜	〜	〜	〜			
[N]	ん	ん	ん	ん			

*《〜》 – denotes a long sound of the character that precedes it. Thus 《ろ》[Ro] becomes 《ろ—》[Rou].

びろ～ん

BIRON

MEKURABE
めくらべ

The Mekurabe is a staring contest embodied in a yokai! It is a chilling entity made up of mounds of skulls and severed heads. These disembodied heads begin as individual skulls that roll around, eventually gathering into a giant, skull-shaped mound. Mekurabe are known for one eerie activity: they stare intensely at anyone who crosses their path. To dispel them, one must engage in a staring contest with this unblinking foe. If you win, the skull will vanish without a trace. If you lose, however, the outcome remains a mystery... as no one has ever come back to recount their fate. Famously described in The Tale of the Heike, the legend recounts how Taira no Kiyomori, a renowned samurai general, encountered a massive mound of skulls glaring at him in his garden. Undeterred, Kiyomori met their gaze with resolve, causing the skulls to dissolve and disappear.

LET'S TRY IT OUT! / やってみよう!

[Me]	め							
[Ku]	く							
[Ra]	ら							
[Be]	べ							

めくらべ

MEKURABE

ASHIARAI YASHIKI

あしあらいやしき

The Ashiarai Yashiki is the epitome of an unwanted house guest—if that guest happened to be a giant, muddy foot crashing through your ceiling! This yokai is notorious for its dramatic entrances, stomping down from the ceiling above and demanding that you clean it immediately. Refuse to do so, and you can expect a temper tantrum of epic proportions, with the foot causing chaos until it's satisfied. This bizarre yokai has haunted many a household, leaving homeowners with one simple rule: always have a towel ready, just in case.

LETS TRY IT OUT! / やってみよう!

[A]	あ			あ	あ		
[Shi]	し	し	し	し			
[A]	あ			あ	あ		
[Ra]	ら		ら	ら			
[I]	い	い	い	い			
[Ya]	や		や	や			
[Shi]	し		し	し			
[Ki]	き		き	き			

あしあらいやしき

ASHIARAI YASHIKI

UONDO
うぉんど

Uondo is a mermaid courtesan, the daughter of the legendary Urashima Tarō, and a carp, known for her striking beauty inherited from both parents. She has a fish-like body with the enchanting face of a courtesan, which made her famous in her time. Uondo married a fisherman named Heiji to help him with his debts, but found her options for earning money limited due to her particularly unique physique. Determined to turn their fortunes around, Heiji and Uondo started a ningyo (mermaid), licking shop, capitalizing on the belief that consuming—or even just licking— a ningyo could grant longevity. The shop became a hit, and they soon accumulated enough wealth to pay off their debts and secure a prosperous future. Despite her unusual profession, Uondo's tale ends better than it started, with the couple living happily and debt-free ever after.

LET'S TRY IT OUT! / やってみよう!

[u]	う	う	う	う	
[o]	お	お	お	お	
[N]	ん	ん	ん		
[Do]	ど	ど	ど	ど	ど

うぉんど

UONDO

TANUKI

たぬき

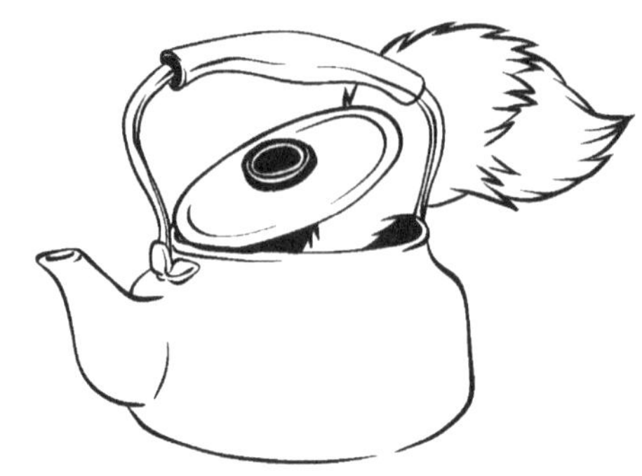

The Tanuki is one of the most beloved yokai known to Japan. A deified raccoon dog, the tanuki has a round body, a fluffy tail, and a jovial, sometimes roguish demeanor. This yokai is famous for its magical powers, which allow it to transform into various objects, animals, and even humans. Tanuki are often seen using their shape-shifting skills to trick people, create illusions, or play pranks. Despite their antics, they are generally considered good-natured and are known to bring good fortune, especially in rural areas where they are believed to protect farmer's crops and the wild nature surrounding it. In Japanese culture, a tanuki is often depicted with a large belly, a bottle of sake, and a set of magical...leaves, that can transform into anything they wish.

LET'S TRY IT OUT! / やってみよう!

たぬき

TANUKI

FUNAYUUREI
ふなゆうれい

Meet the Funayuurei, spectral sailors who redefine the term "ghost ship." These vengeful spirits are the restless souls of those who drowned at sea, and they're not shy about using nautical sabotage to expand their ghostly crew. Shrouded in eerie, luminescent mist, they typically appear on stormy nights during the Obon festival. If you encounter one, be prepared for a ghost ship rising from the depths, intent on sinking your vessel with their large buckets of seawater. Clever sailors counter these spirits by using buckets and ladles with holes to prevent flooding or by boldly sailing through the phantoms—though this daring move could lead to a collision with a very real ship.

LET'S TRY IT OUT! / やってみよう!

[Fu]	ふ						
[Na]	な						
[Yu]	ゆ						
[U]	う						
[Re]	れ						
[I]	い						

ふなゆうれい

FUNAYUUREI

AMIKIRI
あみきり

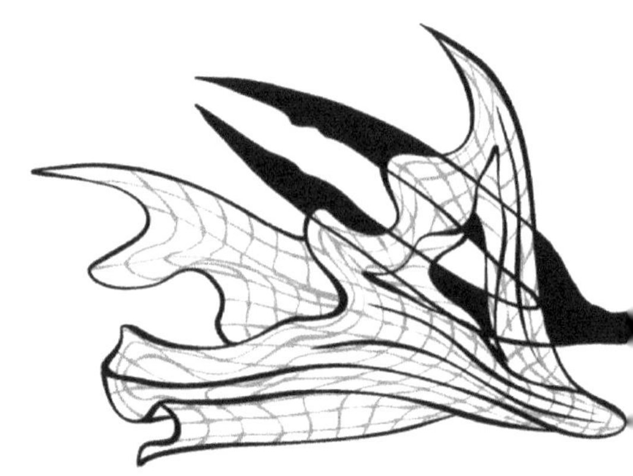

The Amikiri is the yokai equivalent of a mischievous barber—except instead of hair, it's coming for your fishing nets! This shrimp-like creature with a birdish beak is known for its uncanny ability to snip through nets, mosquito screens, or any other pesky meshes. Fishermen have long dreaded the appearance of the Amikiri, as a single visit from this little troublemaker could mean a day's catch slipping away. But despite its pesky habits, you have to admire its dedication to its craft—after all, it's not every day you meet a yokai with such a specialized skill set!

LET'S TRY IT OUT! / やってみよう!

[A] あ			あ	あ	あ		
[Mi] み	み	み	み	み	み		
[Ki] き			き	き	き		
[Ri] り		り	り	り			

あみきり

AMIKIRI

HYAKUME
ひゃくめ

The Hyakume is the yokai that's both an enigma and a spectacle, with a hundred eyes and a penchant for trouble. This eerie entity is a creature covered in hundreds of unblinking eyes, each one peering out from its rotund, mysterious form. Hyakume are nocturnal guardians of old temples, emerging only under the cover of night to keep an eye on potential thieves and troublemakers. During the day, they retreat to dark, shadowy corners where the bright sunlight won't bother their sensitive eyes. These shy creatures generally avoid human interaction but will send a single eye to hover near anyone who comes too close. This eye sticks around to keep watch for any suspicious activity, returning to the Hyakume once it senses no danger.

LET'S TRY IT OUT! /やってみよう!

[Hya]	ひ	ひ	ひ	ひ			
[Hya]	や	つ	つ	や	や		
[Ku]	く	く	く	く			
[Me]	め	い	め	め			

HYAKUME

ARIE

ありえ

Meet the Arie, the ocean's most glamorous fortune tellers in the yokai realm. These aquatic soothsayers are like underwater disco balls, covered in shimmering scales that could make any treasure chest jealous. Imagine a mystical sea lion strutting around on four legs, with a tail that would make even a mermaid green with envy. The Arie is the ultimate VIP of yokai, with only one recorded sighting, making them rarer than a unicorn in Loch Ness. When they do show up, they don't just predict the future—they make it sparkle, scaring away evil spirits with a flair that leaves the ocean's other residents in awe.

LET'S TRY IT OUT! / やってみよう!

[A] あ							
[Ri] り							
[Eh] え							

ARIE

AMABIKO
あまびこ

The Amabiko is a rather charming three-legged spirit that has a knack for popping up just when you need some good fortune. This creature is known for emerging from the sea or rivers, often with a prophetic message—usually about upcoming harvests or, most famously, devastating plagues. Though their appearance might perplex one upon first, second or even third glance, their prophecies have been taken seriously for centuries. In modern times, they've enjoyed a bit of a comeback, particularly during health scares, where images of Amabiko are shared widely for protection and good health. So, if you ever spot a three-legged creature in your local river, don't run—grab a pen and paper, because this yokai's advice could be worth more than gold!

LET'S TRY IT OUT! / やってみよう!

[A] あ			あ	あ			
[Ma] ま			ま	ま			
[Bi] び	び	び	び	び			
[Ko] こ		こ	こ				

あまびこ

AMABIKO

ERITATEGOROMO

えりたてごろも

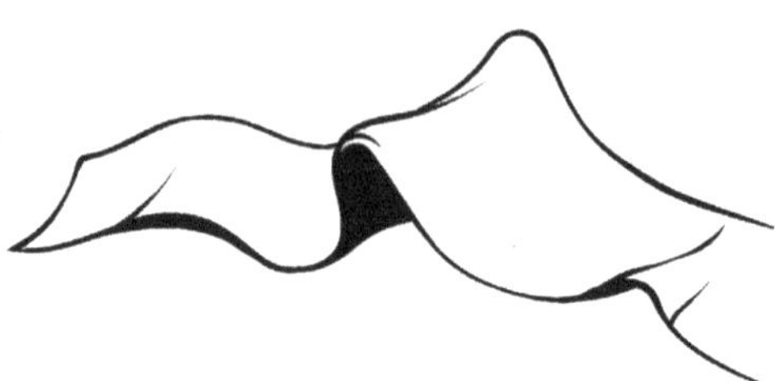

Meet the Eritategoromo, the yokai that proves even spirits can have a bit of a fashion faux pas! This rather peculiar creature is known for its unique appearance—imagine a bizarre blend of a traditional Japanese kimono and a pair of mismatched socks. This yokai is not out to cause harm; instead, it's more interested in making a splash with its unusual look and slightly oddball antics. It's said that the Eritategoromo loves to appear at festivals and ceremonies, where its eccentric appearance and behavior quickly become the center of attention.

LET'S TRY IT OUT! / やってみよう!

[Eh]	え						
[Ri]	り						
[Ta]	た						
[Te]	て						
[Go]	ご						
[Ro]	ろ						
[Mo]	も						

えりたてごろも

ERITATEGOROMO

BEKATAROU

べかたろう

Bekatarou is one of the ultimate pranksters of the yokai world, with a personality as loud as his name. This mischievous spirit loves nothing more than causing a ruckus, particularly by shouting out ridiculous, nonsensical phrases to confuse and annoy anyone nearby. You'll often find him lurking around festivals, where his antics and appetite blend in with the noise and chaos, but don't be surprised if he shows up in quieter places just to stir things up. If you ever hear someone yelling nonsense out of nowhere, you might just be in the presence of Bekatarō—so join in the fun, or cover your ears and wait for the storm of silliness to pass!

LET'S TRY IT OUT! / やってみよう!

[Be] べ	べ	べ	べ	べ			
[Ka] か	か	か	か	か			
[Ta] た	た	た	た	た			
[Ro] ろ	ろ	ろ	ろ				
[U] う	う	う	う				

べかたろう

BEKATAROU

HIME UO
ひめうお

Hime Uo is a mermaid with a flair for both glamour and prophecy. This enchanting yokai boasts the body of a fish and the face of a woman, with a length of about 5 meters long and a massive head adorned in long black hair with two prominent horns. The Princess is not just a pretty face; it's also a bearer of good fortune. Viewing an image of this mystical creature is said to protect against disease and evil spirits. Legend has it that the Hime Uo gained widespread attention in 1819 when a sighting near Hirado in Nagasaki Prefecture led to a flurry of illustrated flyers. These flyers were distributed nationwide, as the Hime Uo's message warned of an impending cholera outbreak and promised protection to those who hung its image in their homes.

LET'S TRY IT OUT! / やってみよう!

[Hi]	ひ	ひ	ひ	ひ			
[Me]	め	い	め	め			
[U]	う	う	う	う			
[O]	お	お	お	お	お		

ひめうお

HIME UO

HOUNENGAME
ほうねんがめ

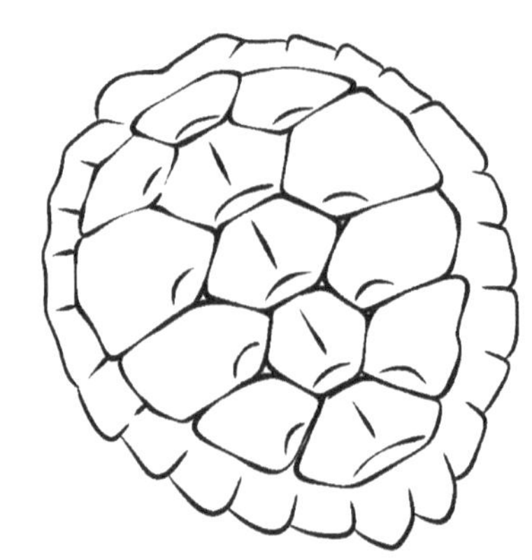

This is the Hounengame, the mystical sea turtle with a knack for fortune-telling. This aquatic yokai boasts a large turtle's body and a human woman's head crowned with long, flowing black hair and often adorned with horns. Residing deep in the ocean's depths, Hōnengame keep a low profile, emerging only when they have an important message to share. Their ability to foretell such events made them highly regarded, and illustrations of Hōnengame were used as protective charms against epidemics.

LET'S TRY IT OUT! / やってみよう!

[Ho]	ほ				ほ	ほ	
[U]	う			う	う	う	
[Ne]	ね			ね	ね		
[N]	ん		ん	ん			
[Ga]	が		か	か	が	が	が
[Me]	め		め	め			

ほうねんがめ

HOUNENGAME

INUGAMI

いぬがみ

Man's best... fiend? The Inugami is the spirit canine with a bone to pick and a reputation that's as complex as its origins. These yokai start off as loyal dogs that, through intense rituals and dark magic, are transformed into powerful and vengeful spirits. The transformation often involves a grueling process that can include burying the dog alive—quite a... wuff... way to become a supernatural being. Inugami are known for their fierce loyalty, which turns into a potent, albeit dangerous, form of allegiance after their transformation. However, they come with a catch: their loyalty is matched only by their desire for revenge if they feel wronged.

LET'S TRY IT OUT! / やってみよう!

[I]	い	い	い	い			
[Nu]	ぬ	い	ぬ	ぬ			
[Ga]	が	つ	か	か	が	が	が
[Mi]	み	み	み	み			

いぬがみ

INUGAMI

YUUREI
ゆうれい

Yuurei are ghostly apparitions found in Japanese folklore, embodying the restless spirits of the deceased who have not found peace. They typically appear as pale, ethereal figures dressed in traditional white funeral garments with long, disheveled hair. Their limbs and body are often depicted as faint and wispy, giving them a spectral, almost insubstantial appearance. Yuurei are believed to haunt the living due to unresolved matters from their past lives, such as unfinished business, unfulfilled desires, or violent deaths. They are most often encountered in places associated with their former lives or in locations where their tragic death occurred. Their presence is marked by phenomena such as sudden drops in temperature, flickering lights, and a general feeling of unease. The concept of Yuurei has deep roots in Japanese culture, with their origins tracing back to early beliefs about spirits and the afterlife. They reflect the traditional Japanese emphasis on ancestral reverence and the notion that certain deaths can leave a spiritual imprint.

LET'S TRY IT OUT! / やってみよう!

[Yu]	ゆ	ゆ	ゆ	ゆ				
[U]	う	う	う	う				
[Re]	れ	れ	れ	れ				
[I]	い	い	い	い				

ゆうれい

YUUREI

IPPONDATARA
いっぽんだたら

This shy little guy, the Ippondatara, is a one-legged demon that's as quirky as it is unsettling. With its singular limb, the Ippondatara hops around in a comical yet eerie fashion, making it one of the more memorable figures in the Yokai Pantheon. Often found deep in the mountains or forests, the Ippondatara would much rather keep to itself than play a prank on some unsuspecting traveler. That is... until the unlucky day of December 20th comes around and this little creature turns indiscriminate and deadly.

LET'S TRY IT OUT! / やってみよう!

[I]	い	い	いい	い			
[pause]*	っ	つ	つ	つ			
[Po]	ぽ	ぽ	ぽ	だ	ぽ	ぽ	ぽ
[N]	ん	ん	ん	ん			
[Da]	だ	ニ	ナ	た	た	だ	だ
[Ta]	た	ニ	ナ	た	た		
[Ra]	ら	ら	ら	ら			

*《っ》 – in some words, a small version of this character exists to denote a pause in between sounds.

いっぽんだたら

IPPONDATARA

ISE EBIZOU
いせえびぞう

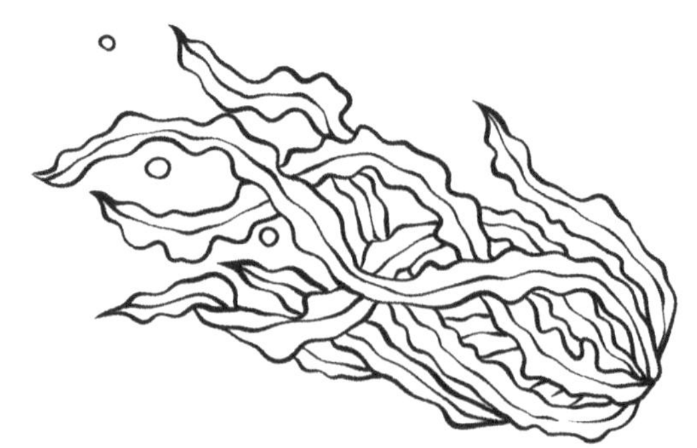

Ise Ebizou is not your ordinary crustacean—this yokai is a striking mix of a spiny lobster and a brave samurai, serving as a noble attendant of Ryūgū, the undersea palace of the dragon god of the ocean. With his tough shell and formidable presence, Ise Ebizou is as much a warrior as he is a guardian of the deep. The character is less of a yokai and more of a cultural development born from a clever play on words, merging the Japanese name for spiny lobster, ise ebi, with the name of a famous kabuki actor, Ichikawa Ebizou. Loyal and courageous, Ise Ebizou served the dragon king faithfully. However, when he dared to speak out against the malicious plots of the king's advisor—an unscrupulous octopus—Ise Ebizou found himself exiled. But fate favored the honorable lobster. When the next king came to power, and the octopus raised an army to threaten him, it was Ise Ebizou's integrity that the young king remembered. With his heroic deeds and samurai spirit, Ise Ebizou remains a symbol of loyalty and justice in both his fantasy kingdom and in the hearts of many Japanese to this day.

LET'S TRY IT OUT! / やってみよう!

[I]	い	い	い	い	い		
[Se]	せ	せ	せ	せ	せ		
[Eh]	え	え	え	え	え		
[Bi]	び	び	び	び	び		
[Zo]	ぞ	ぞ	ぞ	ぞ	ぞ		
[U]	う	う	う	う	う		

いせえびぞう

ISE EBIZOU

ITACHI

いたち

Itachi, known as the weasel yokai, is a small but cunning creature that scurries through the shadows of Japan. As with many creatures in Japanese folklore, Itachi are yokai who were originally your average, everyday weasels! However, they grew so old that they transfigured themselves into a minor deity. In Japanese folklore, Itachi are believed to bring bad luck and even death. They are said to be capable of transforming into humans, using their newly acquired shapeshifting abilities to deceive and manipulate. Some stories tell of Itachi using their sharp claws to attack people, while others describe them as messengers of ill omens, predicting disaster and chaos. Despite their small size, Itachi are respected and feared in equal measure. They serve as a reminder of the mysterious and sometimes unpredictable forces that lurk just out of sight, always ready to pounce from the shadows.

LET'S TRY IT OUT! / やってみよう!

[I]	い	い	い	い	い			
[Ta]	た	た	た	た	た			
[Chi]	ち	ち	ち	ち	ち			
[I]	い	い						
[Ta]	た	た						
[Chi]	ち	ち						

いたち

ITACHI

KAGE ONNA

かげ おんな

Meet the Kage Onna, or «Shadow Woman», who is a mysterious yokai that lurks in the shadows, often appearing as a lone silhouette of a woman cast on a shoji screen. Her form is always in shadow, making her features impossible to distinguish. Despite her eerie presence, The Kage Onna is not known to cause harm. This shadowy presence is often felt in old, quiet houses, where she is said to stand just out of sight, her shadow visible in the dim candle light. Some say she is the spirit of a woman who passed away with deep regrets, unable to move on. Others believe she is a manifestation of loneliness or longing. Though she never speaks or interacts directly, her silent, ghostly figure fills those who see her with a sense of unease, as if she is watching them from beyond the veil of reality.

LET'S TRY IT OUT! / やってみよう!

[Ka]	か						
[Ge]	げ						
[O]	お						
[N]	ん						
[Na]	な						

かげおんな

KAGE ONNA

UMISHIKA
うみしか

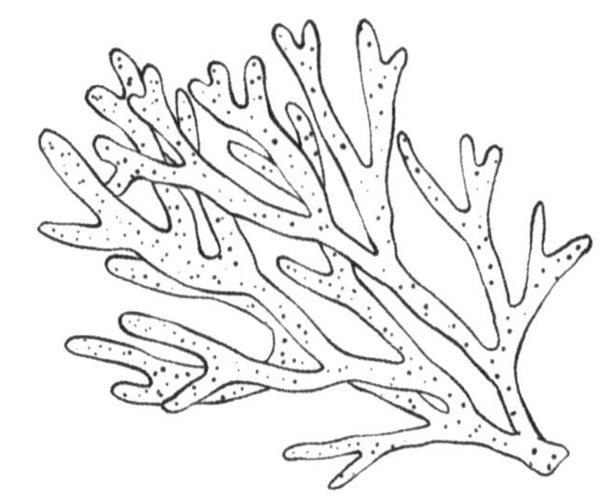

To hunt, or to fish? Well, for the Umishika the answer is a resounding, «yes». This yokai is said to have the body of a deer, but with features adapted to the sea, including scales and fins. It roams the coastal regions of Japan and is often seen swimming gracefully in the waters. The Umishika appears rarely, usually playing in areas where the sea meets the land, such as estuaries or rocky shores. Local legends speak of its ethereal beauty and the gentle, almost hypnotic effect it has on those who catch a glimpse of it. One of the most famous stories involving umishika describes a local fisherman who, while fishing near the shore, encountered the creature. Mesmerized by its beauty, he followed it into the water, only to be led to a hidden underwater realm where sea creatures and mythical beings reside. The experience is said to have changed him profoundly, leaving him with a deep respect for the ocean and its mysteries.

LET'S TRY IT OUT! / やってみよう!

[U]	う							
[Mi]	み							
[Shi]	し							
[Ka]	か							

うみしか

UMISHIKA

KUDAN
くだん

The Kudan is an unsettling yokai that embodies the peculiarity of both prophecies and appearances. This creature is known for its striking form: it has the body of a cow and the face of a human (And sometimes even the reverse!). Legends tell of the Kudan appearing at critical moments in history, often just before significant events occur. Its presence is considered an omen, and its appearance is believed to foretell major changes or calamities. Stories from the Edo Period in Japan describe Kudan sightings linked to times of political and social upheaval, adding to its reputation as a harbinger of significant events. The fantastical appearance of this creature is only diminished by its short lifespan. After its prophecies are shared, it never lives more than a few days.

LET'S TRY IT OUT! /やってみよう!

[Ku]	く	く	く	く				
[Da]	だ	ー	ナ	た	だ	だ		
[N]	ん	ん	ん	ん				

くだん

KUDAN

OBARIYON

おばりよん

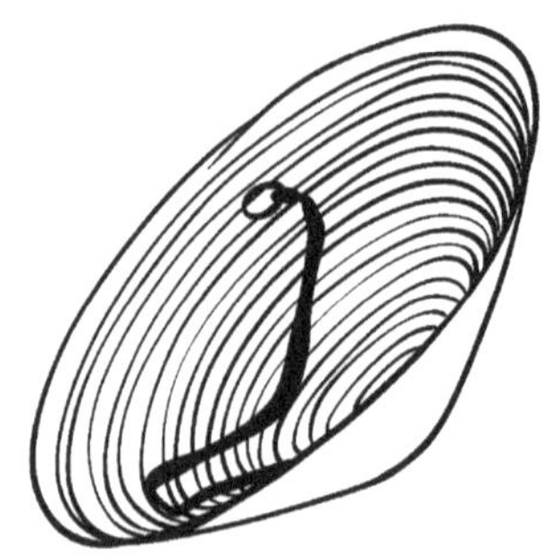

Giddy Up! The Obariyon is a yokai known for its obnoxious ability to become invisible and cause backaches and headaches for anyone unfortunate enough to meet its path. Typically appearing as a small, round creature with a face resembling a traditional Japanese mask, it has the unique power to become unseen by ordinary means. These spirits are infamous for their tendency to latch onto unsuspecting victims and cause them great discomfort. When an Obariyon targets a person, it attaches itself and begins to grow heavier, and heavier, causing increasing physical strain on the victim. The more the person tries to remove the Obariyon, the heavier it becomes, leading to great distress. The Obariyon's origin is somewhat obscure, but it has been featured in various Japanese folk tales and ukiyo-e prints. Legends describe these beings as the spirits of those who have died under heavy burdens, seeking to pass on their suffering to the living.

LET'S TRY IT OUT! / やってみよう!

[O]	お		お	お	お	お	
[Ba]	ば		は	ば	ば	ば	
[Ri]	り		り	り	り		
[Yo]	よ		よ	よ	よ		
[N]	ん		ん	ん	ん		

おばりよん

OBARIYON

TORAKOISHI
とらこいし

Torakoishi, translating to «little tiger stone», is a curious little yokai that blends the features of a stone and a tiger. Found in the village of Ōiso in Kanagawa Prefecture, it appears as a stone with tiger-like features. This quirky creature is not dangerous but enjoys startling passersby. According to legend, a samurai named Yamashita Chōja and his wife, who had no children, prayed to Toraike Benzaiten for a miracle. The goddess appeared in a dream, leading to the miraculous appearance of a beautiful stone. This stone, named Tora in honor of the goddess, eventually grew into a medium-sized relic. It played a crucial role in protecting the samurai Soga Sukenari from an assassin by magically transforming into him. The stone's life-saving legend turned it into a famous attraction in real life. It is now enshrined at Endaiji, where it is celebrated for its protective and blessing qualities.

LET'S TRY IT OUT! / やってみよう!

[To]	と	と	と	と			
[Ra]	ら	ら	ら	ら			
[Ko]	こ	こ	こ	こ			
[I]	い	い	い	い			
[Shi]	し	し	し	し			

TORAKOISHI

KERAKERA ONNA

けらけらおんな

Kerakera Onna is the ghostly figure who haunts the dark corners of Japanese red-light districts with a laugh that's anything but soothing. Known for her eerie cackle, this spectral woman is distinguished by her ghoulish appearance: a rotting face, long, disheveled hair, and a tattered kimono that flutters ominously. Her laughter, which sounds like a series of eerie "kerakera" sounds, is her signature trait, echoing through the night and chilling the bones of anyone who hears it. Those who hear her laugh are said to be cursed with misfortune or impending danger. Her presence is often linked to bad luck, illness, or even death, making her a figure of dread in folklore. Legend has it that her eerie laughter and ghostly form were born from a tragic past, where she was wronged or betrayed. Beware the sound of her laughter, for it is a chilling sign that trouble may be lurking just around the corner.

LET'S TRY IT OUT! / やってみよう!

[Ke]	け				け	け	け
[Ra]	ら		ら	ら	ら		
[Ke]	け			け	け	け	
[Ra]	ら		ら	ら	ら		
[O]	お		お	お	お		
[N]	ん	ん	ん	ん			
[Na]	な		な	な	な		

けらけらおんな

KERAKERA ONNA

KEUKEGEN
けうけげん

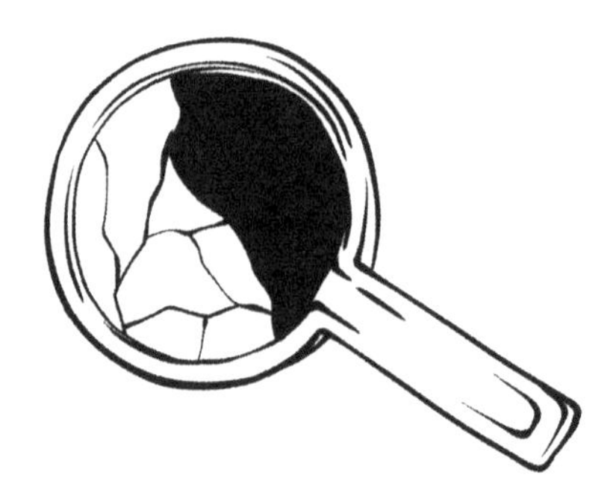

Keukegen is the furry mischief-maker of Japanese folklore, known for its odd appearance and even stranger habits. This small, wild yokai looks like a ball of shaggy fur with a pair of beady eyes peeking out from the mess. Originating from old Japanese stories, Keukegen is thought to embody the spirit of uncleanliness and disorder. Often described as having a rat-like tail and sharp claws, Keukegen is notorious for its tendency to create chaos in households by spreading dirt and muck wherever it goes. Despite its somewhat comical appearance, Keukegen's presence can bring misfortune to those who value a clean and orderly home. It's said that if one encounters this creature, their home will be plagued with unexpected troubles and messes. Its mischievous nature extends to making a mess of personal belongings and generally causing a ruckus in its wake.

LETS TRY IT OUT! / やってみよう!

[Ke]	け	し	に	け	け	け
[U]	う	こ	う	う	う	
[Ke]	け	し	げ	け	け	け
[Ge]	げ	し	に	け	げ	げ
[N]	ん	ん	ん	ん		

けうけげん

KEUKEGEN

KAMIKIRI
かみきり

Bad hair day? Blame it on the Kamikiri, known as the «Hair-Cutting» yokai. It is a mischievous creature that enjoys sneaking up on unsuspecting victims to snip off their hair. This small yokai resembles a humanoid figure with sharp, scissor-like claws and a beak that can easily shear through even the thickest locks. Kamikiri moves silently and swiftly, making it difficult to detect its presence until it's too late. These tricky yokai are often found lurking around bathhouses, weddings, and other places where people let their guard down. They are particularly drawn to newlyweds and women, cutting their hair as a form of mischief. Some legends suggest that Kamikiri also targets those who are about to marry a yokai or spirit in disguise, cutting their hair as a warning to prevent such unions.

LET'S TRY IT OUT! / やってみよう!

[Ka]	か	つ	か	か	か	か	
[Mi]	み	み	み	み	み		
[Ki]	き	〜	〜	き	き	き	
[Ri]	り	り	り	り	り		

KAMIKIRI

JINJA HIME
じんじゃひめ

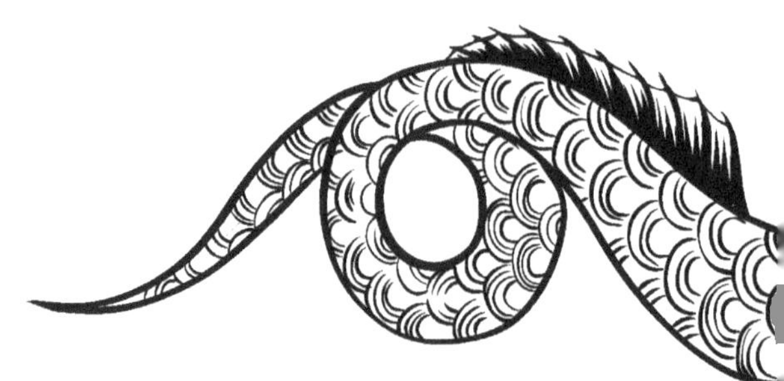

Jinja Hime are mystical beings that resemble mermaids with the body of an oarfish and the head of a woman. These elusive yokai dwell deep within the ocean, far from human eyes, and are known to appear only when they have a message of great importance to deliver from the ocean kingdom below. With their long black hair and delicate features, Jinja Hime radiates an aura of otherworldly beauty, yet their appearances are often warnings of coming disasters. Serving as messengers of the dragon god Ryūjin, Jinja Hime comes to the surface to foretell events such as plagues, natural disasters, or even bountiful harvests. Like many prophetic ocean-dwelling spirits in Japan, their tidings are taken seriously, and images of Jinja Hime are believed to have protective powers, shielding homes and villages from evil spirits and misfortune. These images are often kept as talismans, a reminder of the delicate balance between the mortal world and the unseen forces beneath the waves.

LET'S TRY IT OUT! / やってみよう!

[Ji]	じ	じ	じ	じ	じ	じ		
[N]	ん	ん	ん	ん				
[Ja]	じ	じ	じ	じ	じ			
	ゃ	ゃ	ゃ	ゃ				
[Hi]	ひ	ひ	ひ	ひ				
[Me]	め	め	め	め				

じんじゃひめ

JINJA HIME

KAERU NYOUBOU

かえるにょうぼう

Kaeru Nyoubou, or «Frog Wife», is a peculiar yokai known for her shape-shifting abilities. She often takes on the appearance of a beautiful woman to marry unsuspecting men. In her human form, she is gentle and kind, making her an ideal wife. However, her true form is that of a frog, a secret she carefully guards. Kaeru Nyoubou is known to transform back into a frog when she is alone, sometimes returning to the water to reunite with her kind. In most tales, her true identity is eventually discovered by her husband, often when he sees her shedding her human skin or performing strange frog-like behaviors. Despite the shock and fear that usually follow this revelation, Kaeru Nyoubou remains a loving and devoted partner, illustrating the idea that true love can transcend appearances.

LET'S TRY IT OUT! / やってみよう!

[Ka] か	つ	か	か	か	か		
[Eh] え	え	え	え	え			
[Ru] る	る	る	る	る			
[Nyo] に	い	い	に	に	に		
[U] よ		よ	よ	よ			
	こ	う	う	う			
[Bo] ぼ	い	に	に	ぼ	ぼ	ぼ	ぼ
[U] う	こ	う	う	う			

KAERU NYOUBOU

KATSURA OTOKO
かつらおとこ

Talk about love at first sight! Katsura Otoko is the moonlit enigma who resides on the face of the moon, captivating anyone who dares to gaze up at him. This stunningly beautiful man is said to be so mesmerizing that his admirers find it nearly impossible to look away, even when doing so might lead to their doom. When a person locks eyes with Katsura Otoko for too long, he extends a beckoning hand, luring them closer while their lifespan mysteriously diminishes. If one continues to stare, the danger intensifies—so much so that some viewers might collapse right on the spot, their life cut short by his irresistible allure.

LET'S TRY IT OUT! / やってみよう!

[Ka]	か	か	か	か	か	か		
[Tsu]	つ	つ	つ	つ	つ			
[Ra]	ら	ら	ら	ら	ら			
[O]	お	お	お	お	お			
[To]	と	と	と	と	と			
[Ko]	こ	こ	こ	こ	こ			

かつらおとこ

KATSURA OTOKO

KIRIN

きりん

The Kirin is the embodiment of the majesty of East Asian nature. It is often depicted as a unicorn-like beast with a body covered in glimmering scales and adorned with antler-like horns. The Kirin is a symbol of purity and benevolence, believed to appear only during times of peace and prosperity or to herald the arrival of a wise and just ruler. Its graceful, almost ethereal presence is accompanied by a mane and tail that resemble flowing flames or cloud patterns, emphasizing its celestial nature. In folklore, the Kirin is not only a creature of great beauty but also one of immense virtue. It is said that the Kirin treads lightly on the ground, avoiding even the smallest of living creatures, reflecting its deep respect for all forms of life.

LET'S TRY IT OUT! / やってみよう!

[Ki]	き			き	き	き	
[Ri]	り		り	り	り		
[N]	ん		ん	ん	ん		
[Ki]	き	き					
[Ri]	り	り					
[N]	ん	ん					

きりん

KIRIN

KANASHIBARI
かなしばり

Have you ever wanted to meet Japan's very own sleep-paralysis monster? Well, let me introduce you to the Kanashibari, a phenomenon where a person feels paralyzed and unable to move, speak, or even breathe, often while lying in bed. This terrifying yokai is believed to sit on the chest of its victims, causing this sensation of immobilization. Victims often feel an overwhelming sense of dread and might see shadowy figures or feel a heavy weight pressing down on them. This yokai usually appears during the night, targeting those who are asleep. It is often linked to restless spirits or malevolent entities seeking revenge or expressing their displeasure. The experience can be so vivid that it blurs the line between dream and reality, leaving the victim unsure of what actually occurred. In Japanese folklore, Kanashibari is not just a random occurrence; it is believed to be a form of supernatural punishment or warning. To avoid such encounters, people traditionally perform purification rituals or keep protective charms near their beds.

LET'S TRY IT OUT! / やってみよう!

[Ka]	か	つ	か	か	か	か	
[Na]	な	ニ	ナ	な	な		
[Shi]	し	し	し	し	し		
[Ba]	ば	い	に	ば	ば	ば	ば
[Ri]	り	い	り	り	り		

かなしばり

KANASHIBARI

KOROURI
ころうり

Korouri is a fearsome yokai with a chilling connection to the cholera epidemics of 19th-century Japan. Its name combines the words for «tiger,» «wolf,» and «tanuki,» reflecting its bizarre and unsettling chimeric appearance. Korouri resemble tanukis in shape but are adorned with tiger stripes and possess the menacing jaws of a wolf. These creatures were believed to spread cholera and were often seen in homes afflicted by the disease, feeding on the bodies of those who had died from the illness. After the disease has run its course, they are sometimes spotted fleeing the scene. Their eerie appearance and behavior led to numerous sightings during cholera outbreaks, particularly noted during the 1862 epidemic in Edo. The concept of Korouri, therefore, served as a way to personify and express the widespread anxiety over the cholera outbreaks.

LET'S TRY IT OUT! / やってみよう!

[Ko]	こ						
[Ro]	ろ						
[U]	う						
[Ri]	り						

KOROURI

USHIROGAMI
うしろがみ

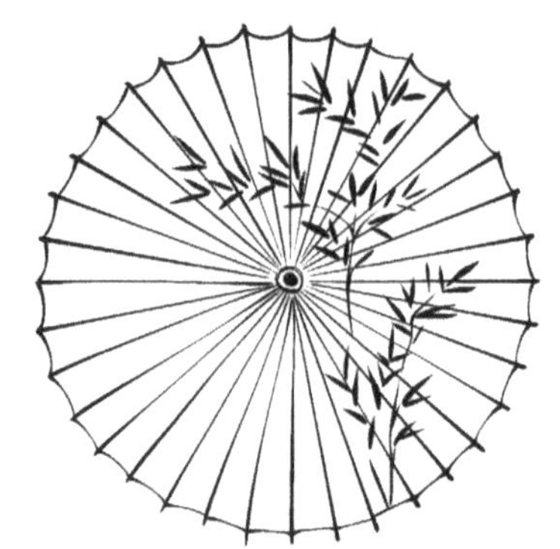

Don't you hate having someone come up from behind and scare you? Well, meet your worst nightmare: the Ushirogami is a ghostly yokai that specializes in instilling fear from behind. This entity is characterized by its long, black hair and a large single eyeball located on top of its head. Lacking feet, Ushirogami has a long, twisting body that allows it to leap high into the air and fly silently. The Ushirogami loves to scare people by suddenly appearing behind them, which is how it got its name. It enjoys tugging at the hairs on the back of a person's neck or touching them with icy cold hands. It also plays pranks by running its fingers through a person's hair, tangling it, or causing strong winds to blow away parasols. Ushirogami particularly target cowardly individuals, often young women walking alone at night.

LET'S TRY IT OUT! / やってみよう!

[U]	う	う	う	う		
[Shi]	し	し	し	し	し	
[Ro]	ろ	ろ	ろ	ろ		
[Ga]	が	つ か	か が	が	が	
[Mi]	み	み	み	み	み	

うしろがみ

USHIROGAMI

YAMACHICHI

やまちち

Yamachichi, or «mountain suckle,» is a rare and curious yokai that resembles a small, human-like creature with a vampiric fixation. Originally a bat, over the years this creature became more and more recognizable for its distinctive appearance: it has a round, pudgy body with a large, mouth-like feature that it uses to «suckle» or latch onto its victims. It is covered in a patchy, bristly fur that gives it a somewhat untamed look. Yamachichi is known for its proclivity to sneak up on people and use its mouth to latch onto their skin, causing a disturbing sensation. It primarily targets sleeping individuals who venture into remote mountain areas, where it uses its ability to blend into the natural surroundings to its advantage.

LET'S TRY IT OUT! /やってみよう!

[Ya]	や							
[Ma]	ま							
[Chi]	ち							
[Chi]	ち							

YAMACHICHI

JOROUGUMO
じょろうぐも

Jorougumo is a cunning and enchanting yokai, part woman and part spider, known for her deadly beauty and deceptive charm. In her human form, she appears as a stunning young woman, captivating and bewitching those who cross her path. However, beneath her alluring kimono lies the body of a massive spider, capable of spinning webs strong enough to entrap even the most formidable prey. Jorougumo resides near waterfalls, abandoned houses, or other secluded places where she can lure unsuspecting travelers. Once a victim is ensnared by her charms, she reveals her true form, paralyzing her prey with venom before wrapping them in silk. Legends say she can control smaller spiders, using them to aid in her hunt. Despite her terrifying nature, some stories depict Jorougumo as a tragic figure, cursed by her nature but longing for human connection.

LET'S TRY IT OUT! / やってみよう!

[Jo]	じ					
[Ro]	よ					
[U]	ろ					
[Gu]	う					
[Mo]	ぐ					
	も					

じょろうぐも

JOROUGUMO

THAT`S ALL!
THANK YOU!
ありがとう!

CHECK OUT MORE OF OUR BOOKS!

LEARN KANJI WITH YOKAI!

Written and illustrated by
Svetlana and Chad Zimmerman

COLORING BOOK
40+ illustrations to color and
words to write in Japanese!

Available on Amazon.com
and other platforms!
ISBN
978-1087869018

MARVELLOUS MIRACLES AND SOMBER STORIES

The Wonderful World of A. Afanasiev

Illustrated by Svetlana Zimmerman

COLOURING BOOK
22 illustrations to color and short Russian fairy stories to read!

Available on Amazon.com!
ISBN
979-8582634959